I0029833

Verax

The Crown and the Constitution

Verax

The Crown and the Constitution

ISBN/EAN: 9783337272739

Printed in Europe, USA, Canada, Australia, Japan

Cover: Foto ©Andreas Hilbeck / pixelio.de

More available books at **www.hansebooks.com**

The Crown and the Constitution.

REPLY OF "VERAX"

TO THE

Quarterly Review.

SEVEN LETTERS
REPRINTED FROM THE "MANCHESTER WEEKLY TIMES."

MANCHESTER: ALEX. IRELAND & CO., PALL MALL.
LONDON: SIMPKIN, MARSHALL, & CO.
1878.

The Crown and the Constitution.

No. I.

APRIL 27TH, 1878.

THE first article in the *Quarterly Review* for April is entitled "The Crown and the Constitution," and prefixed to it as a double text are the titles of a volume of 531 pages and of a pamphlet of 50. The volume is the Third Volume of the Life of the Prince Consort by Mr. Theodore Martin, compiled from materials placed in his hands by the Queen, and prefaced by a letter addressed to "The Queen's Most Excellent Majesty;" the pamphlet, "The Crown and the Cabinet," consists of five letters of mine on the volume just named, which were published in these columns in December and January last. That two productions so utterly incommensurate in bulk and in presumable importance should come to be bracketed together on the front page of the great literary organ of the Tory party is a circumstance which I was not at all prepared to foresee, though I am heartily content to be instructed in the worth of my work by the vehement zeal and the elaborate arguments which are employed to demolish it. When I began writing I never thought of challenging the verdict of so wide an audience. In the discharge of a self-imposed and pleasant duty I merely wrote for my accustomed readers in these northern districts. I never dreamed that the country mouse would visit town. It never occurred to me that my note of warning would find its loudest echo in the metropolis. How could such a thought have crossed my mind? The " Life of the Prince Consort " had passed through the ordeal of London criticism, and been treated, with one or two exceptions, to a shower of compliments. The accomplished politicians who preside over the daily organs of opinion had received it in court attire, and written their eulogies with rose water. I knew the high repute these gentlemen had won as the vigilant guardians of our liberties. I knew how implicitly they were trusted by the public, and how well they deserved the trust; so that if I had thought about the matter I must have felt how visionary any perils would be likely to appear which had managed to escape their skilled and searching glance. Hence the conclusion would have seemed but too obvious that any misgivings I had felt after reading Mr. Theodore Martin's third volume were nothing but the result of a needless brooding over phenomena which a provincial mind was naturally unfit to grasp, and that they would never have been felt at all if I had happened to possess a larger knowledge of affairs, such as is the professional inheritance of political writers who live within three miles of Blackfriars or the Strand. My letters were addressed to a familiar audience, who, if not more on a level with my claims, are at least in the habit of treating them with indulgence, and it was not till they had heard all that I had to say, and had shown that they were stirred by it, that I began to think of sub-

mitting the same thoughts to a larger public. The Reviewer
says I appear to "pose as a tame Junius." If I had thought
of posing at all it would have been as Junius rampant. As
a matter of posing, one would have been just as easy as the
other, and of the two I should have preferred the renowned
original. But the Reviewer does me too much honour. I
thought no more of Junius than of Tancred or of Mungo
Park. The simple fact is that, as an Englishman, my blood
tingled, and I wrote partly to relieve the pain. I have
now some reason to believe that I was right in deciding
to republish the letters. The response has been deep
and wide, and men whose judgment I willingly respect
assure me that some slight service has been rendered to
the State. The *Quarterly* Reviewer says that the "un-
founded opinions" of "Verax" "appear to be entertained
by certain of his countrymen," and that, too, to an extent
which makes it expedient for the champions of the Constitution, as seen from the Tory camp, to buckle on their
harness. I also learn from my Reviewer that " Verax" has
a "following," and that in spite of his "fallacies," perhaps
because of them, he is a representative man. Hence the
heavy-armed battery of fifty pages which has been opened
against "the dangerous fallacies contained in the constitutional theories of 'Verax.'" It is, indeed, a fell and dogged
piece of cannonading, though the cannoneer was too much
flurried to be exact in his aim. The *Standard* imagined
that the aim of the article in the *Quarterly* was to expound
and defend the constitutional theories of Baron Stockmar
and the Prince Consort, thereupon candidly acknowledging

that it took pretty much the same view of Baron Stockmar and his lucubrations as " Verax " did, and was perfectly ready to hand the Baron over to anybody who chose to gird at him. The *Standard* is quite right. Baron Stockmar saw no difference between Whigs and Tories. He looked upon them all alike as weak creatures, capable of nothing better than trading in compromises. He took them all to be unconscious Republicans at heart, not, perhaps, seriously bent upon betraying the monarchy, but at all events practically paving the way for a Republic. The Reviewer handles Baron Stockmar with due discretion. Not a word is breathed against him from first to last, and he is once or twice quoted with an air of benignant patronage, but his constitutional theories are allowed to slumber. The Reviewer, as I shall hereafter have occasion to show, goes quite as far as the Baron, and even further ; but the Baron is not a pleasant man to travel with. The public never took to him, and even Tories eyed him askance. So he is prudently kept in the background. The Reviewer, moreover, appears to lean upon a celebrated Semitic authority on constitutional questions, and has no need of Teutonic guidance. Hence when the *Standard* avowed its readiness to make " Verax " a present of the Baron, the Reviewer wrote at once to say that the gift would do no harm to him. "To a certain extent," so he writes to the *Standard*, "you misrepresent the object of the article in the *Quarterly Review* on 'The Crown and the Constitution ;' the object of the article was to examine, not the constitutional theories of Baron Stockmar and the Prince Consort, but the contention of 'Verax' that the Sovereign could not constitutionally exercise any personal influence in the direction of affairs." To this explanation he is kind enough to add a brief outline of the arguments in the *Quarterly* article, so as to make it easier of comprehension to newspaper people, who are apt to lose their way in intricate reasoning. I may have to avail myself of this help when I come to discuss the theories of the Reviewer, but there are one or two preliminary points which it will be as well to dispose of first. The Reviewer says : "We have been long under the impression that the reign of the present Sovereign has been distinguished by the smooth working of our Constitutional machinery. . . But for the last eighteen months we seem to have been living in a quite different world. There has been solemn whispering and head-shaking in certain circles whenever the name of the Queen is mentioned. Respectable Liberal journals, daily and weekly, have been in a flutter at the aggressive attitude of the Crown." "What, then," he asks, "has the Queen been doing?" and this is his answer: "The head and front of her offending is that she has entrusted to an accomplished man of letters the materials necessary for the preparation and publication of the memoirs of her husband, the late Prince Consort." This he takes to be "an astonishing statement," but says it is "the simple truth," which, however, it may be without being the whole truth. He "reminds" us that the first volume of the "Life" was published in 1875, and the second in 1876, and that when they appeared they were read with eager interest, not merely as containing the memoirs of the Prince Consort, but "as throwing a vivid light on the interior working of our constitutional machinery." He tells us that "not a syllable was breathed by the critics against the character of the Prince Consort or the attitude of the Crown as depicted in this portion of the work. But when the third volume, composed evidently on the same principles as the first two, appeared, there was a loud outcry." He assigns a reason for the different reception accorded to the third volume. It is this: "Whereas a considerable section of the public were vehement advocates of Russia in her recent war with Turkey, the third volume of the 'Life' placed in the clearest light and the most vivid colours the character of Russian diplomacy, the nature of Russian warfare, as well as the anti-Russian sympathies of English statesmen and the English people throughout the events which led to the invasion of the Crimea by the allied armies in 1854." Hence it was thought, he adds, "that the Queen had strong personal inclinations with which she wished her subjects to become acquainted, in order that by the exercise of her Royal influence she might convert the misguided portion of the English people to better opinions. Which exercise of prerogative was, without doubt, highly unconstitutional." There are some deductions to be made from the apparent candour and completeness of these statements. The first volume of the " Life " dealt chiefly with the Prince's early manhood, and closed when the revolutionary movements of 1848 were just commencing. The Prince was new to English ways, and, as the Chancellor of the University of Cambridge and the

patron of Philharmonic Concerts, he ran no risk of offending our constitutional susceptibilities. English politics from
1840 to 1848 were almost exclusively of a domestic type,
but the Prince took a keen interest in German politics, and
on one occasion informed Baron Stockmar that he "had
worked out a plan for the regeneration of the Fatherland,
which he thought of communicating to the King of Prussia."
The Baron was alarmed, and begged him to keep back the
Memorandum, asking, with some pertinence, "Does your
Royal Highness possess the requisite knowledge for dealing
with the subject thoroughly and to the purpose?" Such
incidents were interesting and amusing. The Prince's
Memorandum period was only beginning, and the first ex-
periments were made *in corpore vili.* The turn of English
statesmen had yet to come. The English public laughed
a little, and that was all. The second volume·broke up
different ground, and it had a different reception. Perhaps,
as the Reviewer says, the critics were dumb, but at all
events the public growled. He himself admits as much.
He tells us that the "solemn whispering and head-shaking"
began eighteen months ago—that is, fifteen months before
the publication of the third volume, and immediately after
the publication of the second. The lectures administered
to Lord Palmerston, the right asserted on behalf of the
Crown to read and revise every despatch that was sent out
from the Foreign Office, and, above all, the portentous
Memorandum of Baron Stockmar on the British Constitution, introduced to us by Mr. Theodore Martin in an
attitude of mute and spell-bound awe—these and other

things gave a new and sinister interest to the second volume. There was no loud outcry, but there was plenty of "solemn whispering." The public were indeed alarmed, and their alarm was heightened by the circumstances in which the third volume made its appearance. It was a critical moment. The feeling of a large section of the nation in favour of war with Russia had been mounting higher and higher throughout the year. But the nation was divided. A very large, possibly the larger, section were in favour of peace. Much depended upon the policy of the British Government, upon its wisdom, its calmness, its sagacious self-restraint. Perhaps even more depended upon the moderation of Russia, and that depended upon the absence of fanaticism and passion from its councils. The momentous question for us was whether a divided nation, for the sake of no imperiously pressing interests, should or should not be dragged into a war which might last ten or twenty years, and upset all Europe before the sword was sheathed. Just then the third volume came to us fresh from the hands of the Queen, for into her hands it had been delivered by its accomplished author, and it was from her and not from him that we received it. I need not dwell upon its contents. It is enough to say that a passionate hostility to Russia breathed from every page, that the policy and the diplomacy of Russia were held up in the most odious light, and that the late Czar, with whose son it rested to speak the decisive word for peace or war, stood forth in that volume pilloried by Royal hands as a potentate lost to all faith and honour. I said at the time that the third volume was " a

Message from the Crown sent straight to the nation over the heads of Ministers, and only too well adapted to fire the resentments which those who are responsible for the policy of the country might wish to allay." To-day I repeat the words. I do not say they are true, but I do say that all the evidence forthcoming appears to attest their truth. It had been intended to finish the " Life" in three volumes. The extension of the work to four volumes was an after-thought, and it was resolved upon in order that the exasperating details of the war policy of 1854 might be more fully given in the third volume. My Reviewer says that the first volume was published in 1875, and the second in 1876, as if to show that it was quite in order for the third to be published in 1877; but it is necessary to remind him that the year consists of twelve months, and that an apparent interval of one year may really be an interval of nearly two. In point of fact nearly two years elapsed between the appearance of the first and the appearance of the second volume, while there was only a year between the second and third. The dates of the prefatory addresses to the Queen in the several volumes show this fact very clearly. The date of the first is 20th October, 1874; of the second, 16th September, 1876; of the third, 11th October, 1877. If there had been the same interval between the second and the third volume as there had been between the first and the second, the third volume would not have been published at a critical moment, with the very probable result of exacerbating our relations with Russia, of still further exciting the warlike passions of the country, and of rendering the maintenance of peace impossible. The volume would not have been published till next winter, when it might have been hoped that all danger would have passed away, and the fulminating compounds with which the volume was charged would have exploded harmlessly. Is there not proof enough to sustain the inference that the volume was published when it was with a purpose? Whether there was a purpose or not, the publication at such a moment was indiscreet, and if there was a purpose the purpose was unconstitutional. Published under such circumstances the volume just reminded one of an appeal to the people preparatory to a *plébiscite.* The *Quarterly* Reviewer asks whether we "are to deny to the chief personage of these realms that privilege of free speech which she herself so liberally allows to the meanest of her subjects?" If this statement had the merit of accuracy I should at once profess my infinite indebtedness to the Queen; but even then I should venture to suggest that indiscretion is not one of the prerogatives of the Crown, and that the Queen is as much bound to prudence by the high considerations inseparable from her office as "the meanest of her subjects." There is such a thing as propriety as well as prudence, and, constitutionalism apart, I can discover no propriety in an act tending naturally and obviously to excite the nation to a course of conduct which her responsible Ministers might, on very wise and patriotic grounds, regret and disapprove. The Queen might have done much more on the constitutional theories which the Reviewer propounds, but with these I must deal hereafter.

INSTEAD of disputing one by one the special objections which the *Quarterly* Reviewer raises to the "constitutional theories of 'Verax,'" it will perhaps be more agreeable to my readers as well as to me if we settle ourselves down for a few minutes at the feet of this English Gamaliel, and endeavour to grasp the full meaning of his remarkable utterances. To me, I confess, they have a special attraction. For one thing they confirm my suspicions. In reading the "Life of the Prince Consort" there appeared to me to be traces everywhere of a desire to familiarise us with the principles and the practice of personal rule in matters of government, and to win from us a quiet assent to certain important innovations. The conclusion seemed to be thrust upon us by way of experiment, just to see how it would fall in with our ideas, that the English people had hitherto been living in a state of delusion respecting the functions of the Crown; that the constitutional notions into which we had been born and bred were becoming obsolete; that the reverence we had been accustomed to feel for the High Court of Parliament, and especially for the House of Commons as the collective representation of the whole realm save the Queen and the Peers, was a grovelling superstition; and that to conceive of the Cabinet as of a body of administrators nominated by Parliament, upon whose advice the Crown was bound to act, and upon whose shoulders the entire responsibility rested for everything done whether in home or in foreign affairs, was mere illusion. After going through the third volume of the "Life," I had the impression left upon me that somehow or other the bark of the State was being carried by new currents into unknown latitudes, and that if the hints with which the book was strewn, and the theories which were wafted under our eyes with such an afflatus of Royal approbation, ever came to be embodied in our political life, the future history of this country would be something very different from what it had been for the last hundred and fifty years. I do not know who the *Quarterly* Reviewer is; like me, he is anonymous; but he speaks as one having authority. He seems to have a special mission to instruct us and exhort us and recover us from the error of our ways. Whether he speaks with the sanction of the Crown, or has only stolen the mantle of the Crown's chief Minister, it is at least certain that the literary authority of Toryism is at his back, and that he is enunciating principles which those whom he serves will do their best to carry out. To my great surprise, then, I find him endorsing the inferences which I had distrustfully drawn. I learn from him that my suspicions are all well founded, and that instead of being indulged in as suspicions they ought to be accepted as plain truths, and recognised as the guiding stars of the Constitution. He tells us that in the nature of things government reposes partly upon force and partly upon opinion. Force rests with the father who wields the rod, and constrains his children to obey him. As the children grow up they are likely to have their own ideas respecting the expediency or the justice of frequent whipping, and may even come to doubt whether they ought to be whipped at all. These notions of theirs are the opinion which seasons force. Opinion in relation to force naturally varies a good deal. At one time it may be in favour of abject submission, and at another of wild rebellion; but that government is the best where they are blended with a due admixture; where the Sovereign, who, as the Reviewer tells us, is the " Father of his people," compels or chastises with discretion, and the people, who are his " children," show their good sense by being docile to his authority. This is the basis of the Reviewer's constitutional fabric, and it is duly fortified by a quotation from Aristotle, as well as by sundry awful examples of the evils which happen when the father, who wields the rod, and the children, who have now and then to smart under it, cannot agree as to their respective shares in this disciplinary procedure. The Reviewer traces the fluctuations of force and opinion in the history of the Constitution from the earliest times, and I may have occasion hereafter to take exception to some peculiarities of the process, but for the present it is necessary to follow the main thread of his speculations. In the days of the Stuarts the rod was used too freely. Those eminent fathers of their people, Charles I., Charles II., and James II., instead of giving prudent heed to the voice of opinion, did whatever they listed, trusting too much to the force they wielded as one of their paternal prerogatives. But throughout the drama one redeeming circumstance is to be observed. The Sovereign and the people stood, as they had ever done, face to face. No interloping body of statesmen came between them to moderate the demands of the people and to hold in check the pretensions of the Crown. This evil came in later. At that time regal force and popular opinion fought the battle out, but agreement was found to be impossible, and, as the people were stronger than the King, the King had to go. This was the Revolution of 1688, an epoch to be remembered, since the Reviewer dates from it the commencement of constitutional decay. The Crown was then stripped of the pretensions to personal rule which had led to the mighty quarrel, and tethered fast down to law. The "vast if undefined prerogative" of the Crown, which had been the root of all the mischief, disappeared when William and Mary gave their sanction to the Bill of Rights, and the succession to the Crown was fixed in the Electress Sophia and her descendants by the Act of Settlement. But then, according to our Reviewer, a huge and unprecedented evil stole in. Partly owing to the new maxims established by the Revolution, and partly owing to the fact that the first and second Georges could not speak English, the tasks and the responsibilities of government passed from the Crown into the hands of party, and as the Revolution had been brought about mainly by the Whigs, the party which ruled was the Whig party. The innovation lasted without interruption from 1688 till 1832. George III. strove to emancipate himself from the tyranny of his ministers, and in some measure succeeded, but he was foiled at last, and gave up the effort in despair. To be sure, the Tories came into power with William Pitt in 1783, and had a monopoly of office till 1830, but the damning vice of government by party flourished all the same. For a great part of this long period, says the Reviewer, the Crown was in commission, and throughout the whole of it the Sovereign and the people were kept asunder by interloping parties, who governed in the King's name, and whose right to do so was based upon the idea, derived originally from the Whigs, that it was their duty to defend the people against the prerogatives of the Crown. Political demoralisation was complete. The ancient Constitution of England was over-turned. The people at length actually acquired, so we are told, the habit of transferring to their party leaders the sentiment of loyalty which was due to the Crown. Happily it all came to an end, or ought to have come to an end, in 1832. The people then declared that they could look after their own interests, and the necessity of government by party existed no more. The Whigs expired utterly, so says the Reviewer. Their *raison d'être* was gone. The case was not so bad with the Tories. True, they could no longer pretend to thrust themselves in between the Crown and the people, but they were always the defenders of the Crown, and in the new circumstances their old function revived. The special characteristic of the Tories is said to be this: "So long as the right and honour of the Crown remain intact" they "have not the least desire to restrict the liberties of the people," from which it follows that if the Crown, in the assertion of what is deemed to be its "right and honour," ever comes into conflict with the liberties of

B

the people, it is the liberties of the people that must go. Hence the Tories were well fitted to play an important part in the new state of things which began in 1832. That a new state of things did then begin is of course only the theory of the Reviewer, which I am doing my best to expound; but, without stopping to dispute his accuracy by an appeal to facts which will occur to everybody, let us see what the new state of things is according to his conception of it. In the first place, then, the whole of the period falling between the Revolution of 1688 and the Reform Bill of 1832 disappears from the face of our constitutional history. The mode of governing by means of party and party Administrations, in other words, by means of responsible ministers commanding a majority in the House of Commons, was an unhealthy, irregular, and, judged of by the older practice, an unconstitutional mode of government. It is now at an end, or coming to an end. The Crown and the people now revert to their old relations, such as they were before the Revolution stripped the Crown of its prerogatives. Force and opinion, the rod which coerces and the children who are to be disciplined and coerced, once more stand face to face, with no overshadowing and moderating presence between them. The Queen now appeals to her people, and the people speak back respectfully to the Queen, recognising her motherly affection, deferring to her riper knowledge, and dutifully anticipating her wishes. The doctrine which now rules is that the interests of the Crown and the interests of the people are identical. The Queen holds this doctrine, as I am

sure she does, but so also, we are told, does every
member of the Royal Family. All of them, the Reviewer
assures us, have "shown us how clearly they understand
that the interests of the Crown and the nation are identical."
From this doctrine an important practical inference follows.
If the interests of two parties are identical, either of the two
will promote the interests of the other by promoting his own.
Hence, if the Crown looks well after its own interests, it is
at the same time advancing the interests of the nation.
This is an easy *Vade mecum* for our future kings. They
need not think of the welfare of the nation ; they need only
think of themselves, since this is the same thing as thinking
of the nation. The Reviewer might, perhaps, say that what
he means is that the interests of the Crown, well understood, are identical with the interests of the people, well
understood ; but this he does not say, and could not say
without childishness, for it would be to assert a mere truism,
and to throw open the whole question as to what makes for
the interest of the several parties, and as to who is to be the
judge in matters necessarily and co-extensively common to
both. This last point he assumes to be settled in favour of
the Crown. He maintains in so many words that the Crown
is the best judge of what is best both for itself and for the
nation, and that alike in home and foreign affairs. So the
constitutional pass to which he conducts us is just this.
Constitutionalism, as understood and practised for one
hundred and fifty years by statesmen like Walpole, Chat-
ham, Pitt, Fox, Shelburne, Canning, Wellington, Peel, Grey,
Russell, Lansdowne, and Palmerston, is at an end. We go

back for precedents to the times prior to the Revolution of 1688, which upset everything. The Sovereign and the people, force and opinion, are once more face to face, and are to rule the realm by their happy agreement. Cabinet Ministers are now strictly and literally the servants of the Crown, and may be expected to be at all times willing to adopt as their own the suggestions made to them by the Crown. Parliament will of course assemble as heretofore, but it will give up the initiation of measures and not venture to interfere with foreign policy. As regards imperial politics, it will confine itself to certain vague functions which the Reviewer sums up in the word "control." This will give it more time to attend to Railway Bills and other such matters, and it will probably be able to take more frequent and longer holidays. My readers may ask what would happen if Parliament turned rusty, and whether a debate and a division might not upset this pretty constitutional apple-cart. It is my privilege in reply to point out, always according to my Reviewer, that on the principles which are to preside over the new era this catastrophe could hardly happen. Government, we have already been told, rests partly on force and partly upon opinion, the force being the Sovereign's and the opinion the people's, and these two factors are henceforth to co-operate harmoniously. This harmony is easily to be secured. The rule is obvious. The Sovereign already wields the force of the government; let the Sovereign also dictate to the people their opinions, or rather let them reverently look to him for guidance. In this way they will never be at variance, force and opinion will always agree, and Parliament, which might else prove restive, will merely be the instrument of supplying in the people's name "the spirit and energy that support the head which thinks and the arm which strikes," that "head" and that "arm" being of course the Monarch. The Reviewer tells us that "the Crown is the centre to which all sound opinion, independently of party, should gravitate," and "in the opportunities of collecting, centralising, and directing opinion it is plain that no influence can compare with that of the Monarch." The Reviewer anticipates a natural objection and gives his answer. I quote both. "If it be said that such a constitutional balance would be dangerous to freedom, we answer that, even if it were, it is the natural consequence of self-government under the English Constitution, and, therefore, a contingency which freedom must be prepared to face." He thinks, however, that the danger is imaginary, because the Crown has now no solid support except in opinion, and, of course, if all opinion gravitated to the Crown, and the nation took all its opinions from the Crown, there would be no danger at all. "Finally," says the Reviewer, "if a monarch should ever be blind enough to mistake his interests"—as monarchs sometimes are—"and bold enough to encroach on his subjects' liberties by force"—as a monarch in whom all force is centered, and to whom all opinion gravitates, might, perhaps, be tempted to do—then, says the Reviewer, we should at least be able to fight. I hope we should; but the despotism he advocates often steals like a deadly soporific over the souls of its victims, and kills the virtues which might else arrest its final triumph.   It is safer far to hold freedom fast while we have it than to relax our grasp and suffer it to slip away, or to hold it so loosely and love it so lightly that we hardly know whether we have it or not, and all on the mere chance that, after wilfully losing it, we should be willing and able to wrest it back.   I doubt both the willingness and the ability, except after centuries of bondage and at the cost of bloody revolutions.   History warns us that freedom slighted is freedom lost.   Our Reviewer asks us to surrender it, or, rather, he asks us to believe that it is already surrendered.   His theory is a scandalous fiction; but were it true, or had those in whose behalf he propounds it the power to make it true, we should have to say, as some one said when James I. was beginning to babble his Divine Right notions in the unaccustomed ears of the nation: "If the practice should follow the positions, we are not likely to leave to our successors that freedom we received from our forefathers."

THE announcement made in almost official tones by the *Quarterly* Reviewer, that it behoves us henceforth to look upon the period between 1688 and 1832 as a dropped chapter of our Constitutional history, is of such a startling and amazing description that it almost takes away one's breath. I have réad something like it in Lord Beaconsfield's earlier novels, but that circumstance rather heightens than diminishes one's surprise at meeting with it so many years later in an article obviously not meant to pass for fiction, and within the covers of a perio dical which may pretend at least to the sobriety of age. But there is no fact so strange that it has not an explanation at its elbow. Literature easily acquires a servile taint, and when unscrupulous innovators make good their footing on the heights of power it is seldom long before an applauding chorus is heard from the sycophants below. Our Constitutional history is determined not by what is written, but by what is done. A thing once done is for the time victorious, and all that is venal, or thoughtless, or courtly in the land prepares to follow in its train. Should it prove to be true that we are on the eve of a larger assertion of monarchical pretensions, we may be quite sure that eloquent writers will be ready to prove that what we regard as innovations are but a wise adaptation of ancient maxims to the altered conditions of

the realm. Any doubts that may arise will be referred
for solution to the legal advisers of the Crown, and the
conscience of the Executive will never want the liniment
of plausible precedents, expanded and applied with ripe
sagacity. Should some rash Hampden appeal to the Civil
Courts he may perhaps find that the principles of jurisprudence are not unchanging, and that legal lore can still
furbish up a few weapons in defence of accomplished facts.
We are surprised at being told that the Constitutional
history of the hundred and fifty years ending with 1832 is
an unnatural episode which cannot be too soon forgotten ;
but this only shows what novices we are, and how simple
we have grown through the conviction which has been bred
in us that our liberties are unassailable. If the experiment
now being made upon us succeeds, we may outlive our
simplicity and have to moralise over greater things. Never-
theless, the assertion we are asked to accept is an astounding
one. Let us see what it means. " It is commonly supposed,"
to adopt a phrase which makes my Reviewer angry, but
with which I do not care to dispense, that the period of our
Constitutional history which began with the Revolution of
1688 has been the most glorious in our annals. We refer
to that date our deliverance from a system of government
which was incompatible with the liberties of the people,
with the rights of Parliament, with the independence of the
judicature, and with the dignity of the realm. It was,
indeed, a signal deliverance, and the memory of it has been
embalmed in the gratitude of all succeeding generations.
The evils from which we then escaped had their root

in personal rule. The Kings of the Stuart dynasty could not get rid of the notion that they inherited "a vast if undefined prerogative" which placed them above the reach of legitimate control, and entitled them to do exactly as they pleased. They thought that their power on earth resembled the power of God in Heaven, and was so absolute in its nature that it even set them free from the common rules of morality. They held by this notion with the obstinacy of infatuation. One of them had been sent to the block, but the fiction which cost him his life revived in the breasts of his sons, and in the reaction which followed the extinction of the Commonwealth they almost succeeded in making it prevail. If they had succeeded, England would have sunk into the condition of France or Spain; but happily they failed. The Revolution established the supremacy of law; but it did more than this; it established the supremacy of Parliament. It was seen to be henceforth not so much an axiom as a fact that the will of the people as expressed through their representatives in the House of Commons must be the governing power of the realm. There is but one way in which the will of the people can become the supreme factor in government without imposing too heavy a yoke upon the personal opinions of the Sovereign, and that is by lodging the actual business of government in the hands of Ministers, who can be changed from time to time as often as their policy fails to command the confidence of the nation. The Sovereign cannot be got rid of, and yet the Sovereign cannot be asked to undertake the practical management of measures of which it is not to be

supposed that he can always approve.   Even if we could
trust him to act in good faith against his own convictions,
it would not be decent to exact the sacrifice.   Hence,
from the moment when we resolved that we would govern
ourselves, and not permit any one man, however exalted,
to govern us as he liked, the transference to Ministers
of the work of governing became an absolute necessity.
Nor was it so great an innovation as it seemed; it was
only the systematising of ancient practice.   Distinguished
writers of all countries have exhausted their eloquence
in eulogising this arrangement.   They have seen in it
the highest proof of our political sagacity.   The essence
of Constitutional government has been held to reside
in this, and in this alone.   It appeared to be precisely
what the age required.   Europe had descended from feudal
times crowned or burdened with many dynasties.   The
people, in their ripening political capacity and their growing
love of freedom, wanted to be entirely free, and yet did not
want to part with their Kings.   How should the problem
be solved?   England had shown the way.   Let your Kings
accept as their Ministers the statesmen whom you know
and trust, and whom, on the strength of this knowledge
and trust, you designate for the service of the Crown.   In
this way you may retain your Monarchy and yet govern
yourselves, reconciling by this device the associations of the
past with the demands of a new age.   One of the reasons
why we in England are attached to Constitutional govern
ment is that it enables us to wed the Monarchy with political progress, and to combine with full preparedness for all

the exigencies of the national career the luxury and the satis-
faction of having at the head of the State a descendant of
our ancient Kings.   I have said that this method of government is not a novelty.   The greatest authorities are with me
in asserting that the principles which triumphed at the
Revolution, and are in force to-day, are but a revival of
those which were recognised in early times and were
feeling their way to supremacy under the later Plantagenets,
though they entered upon a long eclipse at the downfall
of the House of Lancaster.   Judged by the result of an
experiment extending through 190 years, they have worked
well for us, and not ill for the Crown.   For that period,
at all events, we have dethroned no kings.   To find
out what they have done for the nation we need only look
around; or if a political proof is wanted, we may compare
the Treaty of Dover with the Treaties of Fontainebleau
and Vienna.   Such is the period we are summoned to
repudiate.   Such are the principles which we are invited to
regard as obsolete.   And we are to go back to what? to
when?   To a system of personal rule, to times of anarchy
and of infamy.   The Reviewer is pleased to pay me a
compliment.   I said in one of my letters that "to provide
against the chance that hereditary descent may occasionally
give us a fool for a sovereign, our forefathers devised the
mechanism of responsible government," and he says, "We
can hardly give 'Verax' credit for being so simple as he
wishes to appear, and we believe he knows very well that
the principle of Ministerial responsibility, so far from being
invented to remedy any weakness inherent in the hereditary

principle, was, in effect, a doctrine founded on the con-
sideration—to use Aristotle's words—'that the power of the
King must be inferior to the power of the whole community,'
and that, like every other Constitutional principle since the
Restoration, it flowed from particular circumstances, and is
sustained by special precedents.   The Constitution is older
than Ministerial responsibility."   I make the Reviewer a
present of the word "devised," and am not sure that I
understand his exposition of Aristotle's doctrine; but on
the question at issue I must persist in being as simple as I
seem to be.   I really hold that the principle of Ministerial
responsibility owes its origin to the necessity of providing
for the "weakness inherent in the hereditary principle."
One would say beforehand that it must be so.   It is not
possible to imagine an intelligent nation undertaking to
allow itself to be governed by the heir whom geniture
chances may equip for the task, except on the understanding that the business of government shall be done
for him by capable persons enjoying its confidence.   The
opposite course is neither natural nor possible, except at
the cost of frequent depositions and at the risk of civil
wars—that is, except by applying the principle of responsibility in the roughest and most direct manner to the Sovereign
himself.   It has sometimes been said that the President of
the United States has more power intrusted to him than
an English Monarch.   The statement is true, and there is
good reason for the difference.   An American President is
elected once in four years by universal suffrage.   He is
usually a man in the prime of life, who has been conversant

with politics from his earliest years. Even if the nation as a whole does not know him, he has been long and widely known by competent judges. He has probably spent some years in the House of Representatives or in the Senate, or perhaps has been a leading figure in the local Legislature, and a Governor of the State. Hence he has proved himself to be a man to whom power may be safely intrusted, and who is likely to use it well. How different is such a man from the babe, or the stripling, or the adult heir who may stand next in the line of succession to an hereditary Crown. Sentiment forbids our setting him aside, and, thanks to Constitutional government, it is no longer necessary; but no one will contend that a nation such as we have become shall deliver itself up blindfold to a ruler whose political capacities have no better attestation than that he is descended from his parents. The "hereditary principle" was not in former times the constitutional principle of the English monarchy. The succession was usually confined to the same family, but not necessarily to the nearest heir. Incapable claimants were set aside, and when the Crown was once conferred possession counted the proverbial nine points at law. But in proportion as the hereditary principle established itself the principle of Ministerial responsibility came in as a counterpoise. I seize the opportunity of returning the compliment of my Reviewer. I can "hardly give" him "credit for being so simple as he wishes to appear" when he gravely assumes that Ministerial responsibility is of later date than the Restoration. He says, as if he were uttering some unquestionable dogma of politics, "the Constitution is older than Ministerial responsibility." I, on the other hand, maintain that Ministerial responsibility is as old as Parliament. As this is not the place for a dissertation on a matter of detail, I must be content to quote an unchallengeable authority. I refer the Reviewer to section 286 of Mr. Stubbs's great work on Constitutional History. He will find the subject of the section described in the margin: "Responsibilities of Ministers insisted on." And what is the period to which the section refers? Well, it includes the reign of Henry III., or let us say, 600 years ago. I quote just one sentence: "The scheme of limiting the irresponsible power of the King by the election of the great officers of the State in Parliament has been already referred to as one of the results of the long minority of Henry III.," in other words of the "inherent weakness of the hereditary principle." But the Provisions of Oxford were adopted long after the King had ceased to be a minor, and by those celebrated acts of State, among other things, twelve Commissioners of Parliament were appointed to manage the Government. So with the Lords Ordainers in the reign of Edward II., and the Continual Council in the reign of Richard II. These were not the King's Ministers, but Ministers appointed by Parliament to take out of the hands of the King's Ministers the work they had done badly. As for the King's Ministers they were repeatedly got rid of by hanging, or beheading, or exile, because, though they had obeyed the King, they had abused his power and misgoverned the people, and because constitutional practice was not yet sufficiently mature to allow of their being got rid of by a vote of censure or by impeachment. And yet we are invited to assume that Ministerial responsibility is a modern innovation subsequent to the Restoration. The Reviewer invites the Crown to resume its former strength, mentioning as an allurement that "strong monarchs have always been popular in England." "The reigns," he adds, "to which the imagination most fondly reverts are those of the First and Third Edward, Henry V., and Elizabeth," but he says nothing about the tragical character of the reigns which followed, though it is surely no trivial matter that the immediate successors of the three first-mentioned monarchs were all deposed and murdered. The power of the great Elizabeth passed into the hands of a weak and foolish man, who held, and no doubt sincerely believed, that to question what a King might do and set limitations to his personal rule was akin to atheism and blasphemy. He narrowly escaped his fate; but his son inherited and fulfilled it. These examples are not of my choosing. They have been selected by a loyal Reviewer for the encouragement of his Sovereign. But I owe to him the opportunity of enforcing by a fourfold lesson the moral on which I wish to insist. The infelicity of personal rule is that it can be bequeathed to a successor only in its weakness and not in its strength. Strong government is possible still, but possible with safety only when the nation governs; and the examples unwarily cited by the Reviewer suffice to show how thoughtless is the loyalty which would urge the Crown to attempt to be strong on any other conditions.

"IT is commonly supposed"—so I said in one of my former letters—"that while the Queen reigns, and all the acts of the Government are done in her name, the responsible business of government, as regards both foreign and domestic affairs, is done by the dozen or fifteen statesmen whom the Queen selects as her Ministers from out of the ranks of the party which commands a majority in the House of Commons." The *Quarterly* Reviewer is very angry with this assertion. He does not attempt to reply to it, nor does he say that it is not true, but he flouts and kicks it like a man in a passion. The supposition itself he ascribes to "ignorance;" for "ignorance," he says, "of the grossest kind it is to suppose that the occupant of the oldest throne in Europe, surrounded by a boundless prestige, possessed of a vast if undefined prerogative, and commanding boundless sources of influence, could ever sink into the capacity of a mere mechanical register of the will of Parliament." Now, whether the supposition itself, as put by me, and not his travesty of it, is true or false, the Reviewer will hardly deny that it is widely prevalent, and this is the pith of my assertion. Nobody imagines that the Queen does the actual work of government, or that she dictates to her Ministers the policy they shall adopt either in home or in foreign affairs. It is a universal belief that she keeps herself aloof from the wranglings of politics, and that, though Government after Government may be swept away, the mortification of defeat and the stigma of popular disapproval can never touch the Throne. The *Times* is a competent witness to English opinion, and I find it within the last few days referring to "the Constitutional theory that the King reigns, but does not govern." The Reviewer ascribes this phrase to "the French doctrinaires," and says that the matter of my pamphlet might be readily compressed into it. Perhaps it might; at all events, I should be content with the epigram, which, moreover, has a more definite parentage than "the French doctrinaires" in general. It was coined by M. Thiers as a terse description of Constitutionalism, and it does not seem to have been accepted by his rival "doctrinaire," M. Guizot. This distinguished statesman was the doctrinaire of another doctrine, which did not work well. He allowed his master to have a large share in governing, and the result was that both master and servant came to grief in February, 1848, when the French nation called them to account. M. Thiers's doctrine might have saved the Throne, but at all events Louis Philippe's practice ruined it. So much for the truth of my assertion as to what the relation between the Crown and the functions of government is "commonly supposed" to be. But the Reviewer says that the supposition itself is based on ignorance, not ignorance as to actual facts, but ignorance as to what an occupant of the English Throne "could ever" become. My readers will perhaps see that in the use of words he is not so accurate as one could wish. Things that are or

c

have been one can know or be ignorant of, but metaphysical possibilities are properly matters of opinion. If I do not agree with the Reviewer as to what an English sovereign "could ever" become, the difference must be set down, not to ignorance on his part or on mine, but to an inability to take the same view of the same facts; and in that case the question whether he is right or whether I am right must be settled, not by mystical rhodomontade, but by sober argument. As to matters of fact it happens that the Reviewer and I are not very widely apart. In my letters on "The Crown and the Cabinet" I gave some reasons for believing that the authority of the Crown had unduly invaded the precincts of the Cabinet, and that in the highest quarters doctrines were held which, if carried out in practice, would seriously conflict with the responsibility of Ministers and with the supremacy of Parliament. The Reviewer seems to admit that what I dreaded has already happened, and he goes so far as to assert that it "could never" be otherwise. With great unwillingness I accept his assertions on the question of fact. We know very little respecting the personal action of the Crown. Between it and us the Cabinet interposes an impenetrable veil. But the Reviewer is perhaps better informed. He may know those who know everything, and thus have a right to be accepted as a messenger from the unseen world. The only knowledge to which I can pretend is derived from the communications which were made to us in the " Life of the Prince Consort" on the authority of the Queen. When the veil was graciously lifted up a little way, apparently for the purpose of tempting a reverent curiosity, and familiarising us with a Court view of Constitutional principles, I ventured to accept the invitation, and turn the rare opportunity to account. The inferences I was forced to draw startled me. I might have hesitated to publish them, since this would be impossible without speaking more freely of the Queen than Englishmen are in the habit of doing; but scruples of this sort vanished when I found that the Queen regarded them with disfavour, and that the custom of suppressing all reference to her in political controversy, instead of being looked upon as a tribute to loyalty, was resented as a device of the Whigs for weakening the Monarchy. Having no desire to incur resentment on this score I spoke out freely, but with due diffidence, not wholly crediting what I seemed to see, and heartily wishing to be set right if my observations had deceived me. In this dilemma I am found by my Reviewer, who rushes in, flushed and flaming, as if from the innermost shrine, shouting to me that it is all true, and that I am a fool for fancying it could be otherwise. Only bethink you, he cries, of the antiquity of the Throne, of its boundless prestige, of its vast, if undefined, prerogative, of its countless sources of influence, and then say whether it is possible for anything short of the grossest ignorance to imagine that the occupant of such a throne "could ever" sink into the capacity of a mere mechanical register of the will of Parliament. An objurgation of this sort, screeched from the lips of a literary apparition, is only too well adapted to flurry a simple citizen like me; but I must do my best to keep cool, and to return to my assailant such answers as I can.

I am confronted, then, with four reasons in favour of absolutism; four reasons all tending to prove, and amounting jointly to unanswerable proof, that the occupant of the Throne of England—that is, at the present time, Queen Victoria—never could and never can acquiesce as a matter of course in the will of Parliament. His first reason is the antiquity of the Throne; it is the oldest Throne in Europe. The fact itself is hardly worth disputing, but there are one or two modifying considerations which ought to be borne in mind for the sake of accuracy. If the Throne of England is unquestionably the oldest now, it is because there has been a great mortality among its possible competitors. Its nearest rival, the Throne of France, has vanished for the present, apparently not to be revived again. The Throne of the Holy Roman Empire went to pieces in 1806. Its fragments were flung to Napoleon and his dogs of war. The Papal Throne has lost its Temporal Power, and is once more what it was in earlier days, the Chair of St. Peter. The extinction within the present century of three of the oldest thrones in Europe might suggest an inquiry into the causes of the relative longevity of political institutions, and the results of such an inquiry could hardly fail to be of service to the next oldest Throne upon the list. But the antiquity of a throne is no reason why its occupant should have absolute power; it is rather a reason to the contrary. Its very oldness suggests the likelihood that it has not, as a matter of fact, possessed that power, for if it had it would have succumbed to the fate, which has overtaken all other

Thrones that have pretended to it, and the lesson of ex
perience is that it never can advance the same pretensions
without tasting the same fate.   The Throne in 1689 was
older than it was in 1489, but it had immeasurably less
power, and only saved itself from extinction by acknowledging the supremacy of Parliament.   The "boundless
prestige" of the Throne, referred to by the Reviewer as
furnishing another reason in favour of absolutism, is, like
all mere attributes, imponderable ; and I know not in what
it consists unless it be in the freedom, the greatness, and
the glory of the nation to which the Throne belongs.   It is
our energy, our industry, our genius, our arms, our blood
that has built up the renown of the English Monarchy and
made it the most famous in the world, and these are not
things to be turned into the price of political servitude.
There are also the sentiments of respect and honour and
veneration which spring up as if by instinct in English
breasts for the person of the Sovereign ; but they are the
fruits of loyalty, they would wither if the roots of loyalty
were to decay, and decay would set in soon enough if the
Sovereign ceased to respect the rights of the people, or
could be suspected of a desire to thwart the will of Parliament.   One has a difficulty in comprehending how this
could be done, but the difficulty does not seem to occur to
the *Quarterly* Reviewer.   He assumes, not only that it is
done, but that it cannot but be done, by virtue of
the regal advantages we are considering.   He shows
great courage in reminding us in this connection of the
" countless sources of influence " which are at the disposal

of the Throne, since it cannot but occur to us that it is by the use of this influence that the apparent miracle of setting aside the will of Parliament is to be performed, if performed at all.   Now we all know that the will of Parliament, when it has once been pronounced, cannot easily be set aside.   When embodied in a Bill which has passed the two Houses, the Royal assent must follow as a matter of course.   On matters of public policy, which are not dealt with by bills, if the House of Commons signified its will by a Resolution or an Address to the Crown, the course recommended must be adopted or there would be a great scandal.   It may be taken as an axiom that the will of Parliament, when once it has been deliberately pronounced, must give law to the Crown as well as to the realm.   Yet the Reviewer scouts the idea that the occupant of the oldest Throne in Europe can ever sink into the capacity of a mere mechanical register of the will of Parliament.   The metaphor is introduced apparently to confuse the issue, which, indeed, he might well be frightened at having raised ; but if he means anything it must be this—viz., that the Sovereign is able to evade compliance with the national will as expressed through Parliament.   The Reviewer puts us in a dilemma, and we are compelled to feel our way out of it as best we can.   We know full well that the will of Parliament, when it has been formally pronounced, cannot be evaded, and yet we are told that it is evaded.   How can that be ?   It is not, perhaps, altogether a matter of chance that the Reviewer brings together in this connection two such words as "influence" and "will."   The

" will" of Parliament is made up of the wills of the majority of its members, and " will " is the field of " influence." A given state of the will, as metaphysicians call it, is the result of given motives presented to the mind, and its contents would have been different if the motives had been different. Hence, though the will of Parliament cannot be evaded, it can be controlled. Instead of leaving it to shape itself, it is possible to help in the shaping of it; and the person who is able to do this, though obliged to acquiesce in the decision when it has once been pronounced, is no " mere mechanical register" of the decision, but its originator. This, according to our loyal Reviewer, is what the Crown is doing, and, if done, it can be done only in two ways : either by appealing to the people, and so helping to form the opinion which Parliament represents, or by influencing those who wield the opinion of Parliament. Our constitutional arrangements lend themselves most readily to this latter method. To secure the host, it is enough to secure the leaders. The will of Parliament is the will of the party majority, and so long as the party submits to be led by its chiefs the power that controls them controls Parliament. We are thus led back once more into that mysterious region where the pasture lands of the Cabinet break away into the highlands of the Crown, and where " countless sources of influence" give forth their fertilising streams. In this happy region open the golden gates which give access to the upper grades of our social hierarchy, where the glorified Commoner assumes the coronet and begins his heavenward ascent. Here are the prizes of parliamentary struggles and magnanimous self-surrenders, and here, perhaps, sometimes, among nobler aspirants, the subservient Minister grasps his high reward, and settles down among the Peers of England, whose historical renown becomes the price for which a nation is mystified and its confidence betrayed.

In my last letter I referred to some of the reasons which, in the opinion of the *Quarterly* Reviewer, make it utterly absurd to suppose that an English Sovereign " could ever " submit as a matter of course to the will of Parliament. The reasons I then touched upon were the antiquity of the Throne, its boundless prestige, and the " countless sources of influence " which are at its disposal. But the Reviewer mentioned a fourth reason, viz., the possession by the Sovereign of " a vast, if undefined, prerogative," and this appeared to be so important that I decided to reserve it for a separate discussion. In his letter to the *Spectator* of May 4th, he dwells afresh upon " the actual existence of the Royal prerogative." " Whether you and ' Verax ' like it or not," he says to the editor of that journal, " you are con- fronted with the fact of a Royal person in possession of very extensive powers;" and a little further on he speaks of " the Royal person aforesaid " as " possessed of a vast legal prerogative." He seems, indeed, to recognise but two factors in the Constitution of to-day—Royal Prerogative and Public Opinion ; and he says that the great question to be settled is " how these two distinct but not necessarily antagonistic forces are to be reconciled with each other." To his apprehension Parliament does not figure separately in the problem. Parliament is not so much an institution as a branch of public opinion, and public opinion is the real rival of Royal prerogative. But having brought these two powers face to face with each other, he proceeds to knock one of them to pieces. One half of his article in the *Quarterly* is devoted to an attempt to prove that public opinion is but a poor judge of domestic questions, being oftener wrong than right, and that in foreign questions it is utterly incompetent. He assures us, almost in so many words, that public opinion is generally a dolt or a fool, and if so the conclusion is plain. Once admit that the welfare of any concern depends exclusively upon the intelligence of two persons, one of whom is a fool, and it follows that the concern will fare badly unless the person who has some intelligence is allowed to do as he likes. This being the Reviewer's conception of the relation in which the Royal prerogative and public opinion stand to each other, it is clearly his view that the welfare of the nation depends upon the unfettered exercise of the prerogative. Public opinion, so he says, though it is the informing spirit of Parliament, is seldom to be trusted. Our one true and safe guide through the thorny labyrinths of public affairs is that Royal person who is likelier than any or than all of us to know what is best; whose judgment no passion ever clouds; and whose prerogative, equal as a separate force to the rival force which resides in the nation, has over it the enormous advantage of being always intelligent and always wise. This is the Reviewer's estimate of our position, but knowing, as we do, to what baleful ends some of our kings have used their prerogative, we may be pardoned if we cannot persuade ourselves to trust it any more than he trusts public opinion; and so, putting his pessimist views and ours together, it may well be a matter of wonder how the nation has managed to survive so long. My explanation of the matter is that we have kept prerogative well at bay. Our fore-fathers seized it and bound it, as the Angel in the Apocalypse did with Satan, that it might harm us no more. The nation has prospered in proportion as it has been allowed to govern itself. Often well-nigh ruined by prerogative, it has as often raised itself from the dust by its own energies, and, after giving a final throw two hundred years ago to the oppressive power of its monarchs, it entered upon a perpetually extending domain of freedom and prosperity. But what is the Royal prerogative? Let us approach it with due respect, but not with unsandalled feet, and ask with fearless curiosity wherein it consists, and what is the nature and what the basis of the rights which are so mysteriously asserted over us on its behalf. Our Reviewer gives us no help in this inquiry. He says that prerogative is "vast" and "undefined;" and vast anything must be which has no definition, and so can have no *finis* put to it. I do not want to weary my readers with a dry disquisition, but I must run the risk, in order to convey to them some notion of what prerogative is understood to be, and of the way in which it has grown up. The thing itself, as the Reviewer truly says, is "undefined;" never-theless some attempts have been made to define it. Sir Henry Finch, writing in the palmy days of Charles I., says

it is " that law in case of the King which is law in no case
of the subject." Blackstone obliges us with a description
instead of a definition. " By the word prerogative," he
says, " we usually understand that special pre-eminence
which the King hath over and above all other persons, and
out of the ordinary course of the common law, in right of
his regal dignity. It signifies in its etymology (from *præ*
and *rogo*) something that is required before or in pre-
ference to all others; and hence it follows that it must be
in its nature something singular and eccentrical." This
luminous explanation does not entirely disperse the gloom
which surrounds the subject, but if we carry with us the
idea that the prerogative is " something singular and
eccentrical," it will be no bad guide. For a definition
grounded upon facts we must come to Hallam, who tells
us that " prerogative in its old sense might be defined as
an advantage obtained by the Crown over the subjects, in
cases where their interests came into competition, by reason
of its greater strength." This hits the mark. We must
conceive of two powers confronting one another—a King
who wants to have as much of his own way as he can get,
and a people conscious of their rights and anxious to assert
them. The King is one, the people are many. His counsels are united, theirs divided. He has " countless sources
of influence " at his disposal, big slices of folkland to give
away and earldoms to bestow, and so can induce others to
make common cause with him and fight for him, whereas
they for the most part are poor and helpless. Perhaps no
open struggle ensues. In ordinary times the conditions of

the case would hardly admit of one. But from year to year, and from century to century, successive kings watch their opportunities and make the most of them, and all the power they can wrest to themselves out of the helplessness of their subjects, all the advantage they can win by fraud or extort by force, they appropriate as theirs for ever, and style it their " prerogative." In the course of time, by an irony which becomes the strong, they pretend that their prerogatives were given to them for the good of their subjects. " I must confess," says Hallam, " that no part of this assertion corresponds with my view of the matter. It neither appears to me that these prerogatives were ever given, nor that they necessarily redound to the subjects' good." No; they were never given. They were seized upon and held by the right of the strongest. It is one of the most curious things in the world to observe how these stolen rights—for such they were originally—became gradually transformed into sacred prerogatives, and gathered upon them the dews of heaven. As one element in the process must be reckoned the influence of the Church. It would be a mistake to suppose that the Church in the Middle Ages favoured the absolute power of kings. The Church had pretensions of its own which brooked no secular rival, but one thing at least it did for kings—it conferred upon them the sanctions of religion. Anointing oil was first used at the coronations of the Eastern Emperors at Constantinople, and it soon made the tour of the West. When the bishop poured the sacred oil upon the monarch's head, people bethought themselves of the prophet Samuel, who in this way singled out David as the chosen of the Lord, and anointed him to be King over Israel. Henceforth the new King was the Lord's Anointed, upon whom it was impious to lay hands, and whose authority—all that he had yet gotten to himself, and all that he still hoped to get—could be held out as in some sense the gift of Him by whom kings reign and princes decree justice. Next to the Church, as the instruments by which regal rights were transformed from robbery to prerogative, must be placed the lawyers, most of whom were clergymen employed in civil functions. In the thirteenth and fourteenth centuries there was a great revival in the study of Roman law, founded on the Institutes of Justinian. As the grandest and most symmetrical system of jurisprudence ever created, it naturally took possession of the legal intellect of Europe ; and, though it was never formally brought into use in this country, there can be no doubt that its maxims very largely influenced the reasonings of English lawyers. It soon became the object of law writers to systematise the English law after the fashion of the Roman law, to trace it down to first principles, and give to every part of it, as far as possible, a *raison d'être* in the nature of things. They did this for the regal power, taking as their guide the Imperialism of the Roman law, and a very fine theory they turned out. I take it that most of these law writers were skilled in the scholastic logic of the day, and that they did for monarchical doctrines pretty much what their compeers in another line of thought did for theology. At all events, the distinctions which were drawn between

the personal and the political capacity of the King, and
the definitions given of the various ways in which one
of these capacities affected the other, involved a tissue
of metaphysical refinements that would have done credit to
Anselm or Aquinas. By the end of the Middle Ages the
metamorphosis was complete, and the prerogatives of the
Crown figured in the redoubtable and sacred character
which they have worn for some eyes ever since. By that
time it could be gravely asserted that, while all men were
subject to the King, the King was subject to none but
God; that everything a subject possessed belonged by right
to the King, to whom it pertained to take just so much as
he wanted, and of his grace and favour to leave the rest ;
that Parliaments owed all their privileges to the King's
goodness, and that when he pleased he could resume them ;
that the judges were only his delegates, and that, as a principal can always take the place of his agents, so the King
can, if he pleases, take the place of his judges, and give
such decisions as he sees fit ; that as all laws are made
by his delegated authority, he can suspend laws, or issue
proclamations which will serve as well as laws ; that all
power proceeds from the King ; that he can do no wrong ;
that he cannot even imagine wrong ; that he is personally
present in all his courts of justice; that he is never a minor;
that he never dies, together with a host of similar fictions
and extravagances. Be it well understood that no statute
ever sanctioned these conceits, and that they are unknowr
to the ancient Common Law of England. They owe theil
origin to the systematising ingenuity of the writers of law

books, though kings and sycophant ministers gladly laid hold of them for their own purposes. Some of these high-flown fictions have been turned by forensic and political alchemy to honest uses. If the King cannot imagine what is wrong, it is certain that he cannot intend what is wrong, and an upright judge could, therefore, reverse in the King's name a wrongful decision pronounced by the King himself, or under his directions. In the same way, if the King can do no wrong, it is obvious that his public acts must be done for him by persons who can raise no such presumption in their favour—a necessity which leads straight to responsible government. But though these fictions have been rendered harmless, they show what a dangerous proneness there once was to an idealisation of the person of the Sovereign, and how narrowly we escaped that Oriental submissiveness which first deified and then destroyed the Monarchy of France. It is much to be wished that the friends of pre-rogative at the present day would tell us more about it than they do. On this high theme we ought not to be left to gather our information from reverential glances and mysterious allusions. If the Crown has any rights which can be exercised in opposition to the will of Parliament, I should like to see them scheduled; or if the Crown has any rights which cannot be exercised now, but are to be considered as latent and held in suspense, ready to be asserted as soon as the authority of Parliament can be successfully evaded, in that case also it is very desirable that a list of them should be made out by some competent hand. If the struggles of the seventeenth century are to be renewed, it is high time to survey the battle field and prepare for the onset. Watchfulness is the more necessary because the Constitution is not likely to be openly assailed. Should an inroad be attempted, it will probably start from some familiar maxim, and the innovation will wholly consist in giving to the maxim in question a narrower or a wider meaning than is consistent with its spirit, or than those who framed it would have sanctioned if they could have foreseen the altered circumstances of to-day. Within the past week we have had examples in both directions. Two hundred years ago it was laid down that a standing army was not to be maintained in this country in time of peace without the consent of Parliament, and that the Crown ought to have the absolute disposal of the military forces of the Crown. If we are to accept the contention of the Attorney-General, the first of these maxims is to be narrowed so as to apply only to the United Kingdom, while the second is to be extended so as to include the military forces of India. The India Act of 1858, as it passed the House of Commons, contained a clause which would have prevented the Crown from employing the Indian Army out of India without the consent of Parliament; but it was alleged that this clause limited the prerogative of the Crown, and a new clause was introduced which shifted the incidence of the prohibition from the use of Indian troops to the use of the funds of the Indian Treasury for supporting them. We have probably not heard the full history of this substituted clause. On the plea of saving the prerogative of the

D

Crown as regards the disposal of its military forces, the clause gave to the prerogative a wide and dangerous extension, as we are now finding out, and may find out more fully some years hence, when Europe has fully mastered the portentous fact that the shores of the Mediterranean may be menaced any moment by a Sepoy army. The tenor of the substituted clause was well remembered by those who sent the secret orders to India six weeks ago. As regards the older prerogative, there is no mystery about it. History shows us a time when it did not exist at all, and it also tells us, if not how it grew, at all events that it did grow, bit by bit, till at length the elected chief of a band of pirate emigrants was changed into a Heaven-anointed King, great in the privileges allowed to reside in him, but greater far in the fund of latent claims which lay behind the throne, and which he sought to enforce as often as he found opportunity. What we have to remember is that the principles of English liberty are older than the prerogative. They existed before the prerogative—in the dimensions it ultimately assumed— was ever dreamed of, and the history of their development, from the period, not of their birth, but of their resuscitation, in the days of Magna Charta, down to the Revolution of 1688, was the history of an incessant and ultimately victorious struggle against the pretensions of the Crown. The prerogative, "vast if undefined," which the *Quarterly* Reviewer brings out of the seclusion of two centuries and expects us to worship, we know only as the persistent enemy of freedom, and an attempt to restore its ascendency would be fitly met by recurring to the glorious examples of our ancestors. Save that fragment of it which is embodied in Parliamentary Statutes, or survives in continuous usage, and is practically identical with the discretion reposed by Parliament in the responsible Ministers of the Crown, prerogative is dead. The Bill of Rights and the Act of Settlement, the title-deeds of the reigning dynasty, are monuments built upon the grave of prerogative, and any Minister who sought to revive it would deserve to be reputed a traitor alike to Queen and People.

IN the course of these letters I have often had to refer incidentally to the doctrine held forth by the *Quarterly* Reviewer respecting the functions of the Crown in the management of foreign affairs, and before bringing them to a close it may be as well to dwell a little more fully upon a question which has lately excited so much concern. In my remarks on Mr. Martin's " Life of the Prince Consort" I ventured to assume that foreign affairs are as truly the affairs of the nation as home affairs, and that the nation is as much entitled to decide upon the line of conduct to be pursued towards other nations as it is to make its own laws or to settle the principles of its internal administration. In the opinion of the Reviewer the nation ought to confine its attention to domestic affairs, and leave foreign affairs exclusively in the hands of the Sovereign. Parliament is invited to remember that it is only a part of the Great Council of the Realm, and that in regard to foreign questions its proper province is control. To frame a right course of action in foreign affairs is said to require qualifications which Parliament does not possess. For one thing it is destitute of the requisite knowledge. Average Englishmen, we are told, know but little of the geography, the history, or the resources of foreign States, and the odds are that the men they choose for their representatives do not know much more. Parliament does not number Emperors and Kings among its personal acquaintances; it has no experience in the mysteries of diplomacy, and no means of forming alliances. Foreign potentates know nothing of Parliament except as one of the domestic institutions of the realm. "Our constitutional arrangements are nothing to them." They recognise the Queen as the "visible representative of the national majesty." They deal with her as if she were as absolute as themselves, and hold her responsible for the nation. Unless we abandon all transactions with these august personages, we must, therefore, so it is said, conform ourselves to their ideas of government, and give to the Queen that absolute power without which she cannot act with firmness, nor assure herself of being able to carry out a consistent policy. Parliament, moreover, so we are confidently assured, has not the means of giving effect to its decisions on foreign affairs, were it rash enough to form any. It rests with the judgment of the Queen to decide upon peace and war, and the movements of the military forces of the country depend upon her will. Mere Englishmen have only to think of the security of their country, but the Queen has also to think of her own honour, and this gives her a double interest. Hence, says the Reviewer, her interest in foreign questions is "beyond comparison greater than that of any other single Englishman, and may even be compared to that of the nation itself." Hence the Queen is at once "the head and the arm of the Constitution," the intellect that guides and the sword that defends the realm. It follows that there is but one rule for

Englishmen in reference to foreign questions. They are asked neither to think nor to decide. This is not their business. All they have to do is to give "generous and ungrudging support to the Sovereign power," understanding by "Sovereign power," not Parliament, in which, according to the great expounders of the Constitution, Sovereignty alone resides, but the person of the reigning monarch. The Reviewer says that "when the Romans had acquired empire, and found that their old constitutional machinery was inadequate to the administration of their affairs, they deliberately chose to retain empire at the cost of liberty." He hints that this choice will not be ours, but that we shall show that we know "how to maintain both liberty and empire, by placing full confidence in the Sovereign." But this seems to be precisely what the Romans did. Instead of asserting the authority of the Senate in the management of affairs which embraced the whole of the civilised world, they "placed full confidence" in their Imperator, and lost their liberty. It is odd that we are recommended to take the same course to preserve ours, and I for one should like some better guarantee for the success of the experiment. But if Parliament were ever so well qualified to meddle with foreign affairs, the Reviewer assures us that there would be a fatal objection to its doing so in its want of adequate leisure. We are told that it "groans under the weight of the duties with which it has charged itself since it abandoned its old functions of control to take the initiative in legislation," and that "it becomes every year more incapable of accomplishing the task which its ambition has undertaken." At every turn in the discussion the Reviewer treats us to a fresh surprise. "The initiative in legislation" is, it seems, a function which does not properly belong to Parliament, and the magnitude of its legislative work is only an instance of its "ambition." Under the new state of things for which it is the mission of the Reviewer to prepare the way, we may infer that the sole right of introducing bills will be transferred to the Crown, and that most of the business which now occupies the time of the Legislature will be discharged by one of Her Majesty's principal Secretaries of State, with no other help than a body of clerks and the seal of the Department. But, as things are now, even the omnivorous activity of Parliament cannot dispose of all the work that has to be done. The "architecture of the State" needs to be made "worthy of the State's imperial character," our rivers want purging "of the acids by which they are poisoned,'" and the features of a once beautiful country preserved "from the plague of smoke by which they are disfigured." Hence, even if Parliament could pretend to rival the sagacity of the Crown, it would still be necessary to institute a division of labour; and, that being the case, what arrangement could be better than that Parliament should give the whole of its time and attention to domestic legislation, and leave the domain of foreign affairs in the hands of the Sovereign? The business of the nation would then be properly conducted; the representatives of the people would look after dirty rivers and smoky chimneys, and the Crown would settle whether there should be peace or war. In speaking of the Crown we usually understand by it the Crown in its political and impersonal capacity, but the Reviewer means by it the personal rights of the Sovereign. He demands for the Queen a "large personal share in the control of our foreign policy," and declares that it belongs to her, not only "by virtue of her prerogative," but "by the nature of things." What is demanded for the Queen is demanded, of course, for her successors. The Reviewer marks with a *sic* my reference to "hereditary brains," but the phrase is sufficiently accurate to point a pertinent question. Granting that we may safely entrust the foreign policy of England, with all the momentous issues that depend upon it, to the "personal control" of the Queen, what guarantee can we possibly possess that the calm intelligence, the freedom from prejudice, and the capacity for patriotic self-detachment for which she is distinguished, will be possessed in an equal degree by those who come after her? For the competence of a Cabinet we have some approach to a guarantee in the voice of the nation and the votes of Parliament ; but what guarantee can we ever have for the competence of successive wearers of the Crown? If a Cabinet blunders it can be dismissed, but if a Sovereign blunders the Constitution affords us no remedy. The inference suggested by common sense is that the Sovereign cannot be intended to occupy a position in which blundering is possible, whereas our Reviewer would have us adore her blunders, and still go on reposing in her the blind trust which appears to be demanded " by the nature of things." It is now time to bestow a glance upon some of the larger reasons which the Reviewer advances in support of his doctrine, and the first is that the doctrine itself is a faithful record of our immemorial practice. Foreign affairs, he says, were always regarded as the private domain of the Crown, and in this fact we have the origin of our political liberties. This part of his argument is a curious tissue of misstatements and fallacies, and I must do my best to disentangle it. We are told that at an early period in the history of the nation the monarch and the people were united in a common bond of self-defence " by the attitude which the Crown assumed in its foreign relations in consequence of the insular position of the kingdom." "The English people," we are further informed, "have always instinctively understood that the maintenance of their domestic liberties depends on the independence of their country, and they have naturally looked for the preservation of this independence to their Sovereign as the depository of the concentrated force of the nation." It does not need much instinct for a nation to know that if they are to retain their freedom they must not allow another nation to become their masters ; but it is puzzling to make out how " the insular position of the kingdom " made it specially difficult for the English people to maintain their independence. That circumstance, one would say, should have made the task easier. Then, as to our political liberties. They were won, says the Reviewer, from our monarchs by a process of bargaining. As often as the monarch wanted to go to war, his people refused to supply him with the means of warfare unless he made them some concession. Thus we have the highly singular spectacle of a people who "instinctively understood" that their independence could only be preserved by the warlike attitude of the Crown, but who yet, whenever the monarch wanted to fight for them, instead of applauding his resolution as a proof of patriotism, and flocking gratefully to his standard, coolly seized the opportunity for striking a bargain. Our forefathers were shrewd men, to say the least ; and the "bond of union " between them and their monarchs was so lax that it permitted the two parties to aim at different ends, and to higgle with one another on the way to the battle field. These statements are incongruous because they miss the truth. The Reviewer may not wish to mislead, but he has to make out a case, and such a purpose is not favourable to accurate history. The truth is that our insular position was always favourable to national independence. If the English Channel had been dry land we should have been swallowed up in the empire of Charles the Great, and become, a few centuries later, one of the fiefs of the French monarchy. But the ocean served us as a rampart against the invader. Our national independence was secure in its sea-girt home. Our kings went to war, not to maintain our independence, but to prolong their own sway over their continental dominions, or to reconquer them after they had been lost, and so far from securing our national independence by these exploits they did all that lay in their power to endanger it. These continental complications lasted from the Norman Conquest to the loss of Calais, a period of nearly 500 years. Englishmen were then pretty much what Englishmen are now, fond of glory and fond of fighting. Still, as the cause was their monarch's more than it was theirs, they made him pay for their assistance, and the cost of war became the purchase money of freedom. The people never did make, and never would have made, a battle for independence the subject of a bargain. As events turned out, the military exigencies of the monarch were favourable to self-government, but it is a fiction to suppose that national independence was the prize of warfare. The French people could have told a different tale when their lands were wasted with fire and sword by English invaders, and an English King was crowned in Paris. But our forefathers were wiser than their children. They made the warlike projects of the Sovereign the means of extending their liberties, whereas we make them the occasion of surrendering ours. Another reason why we are said to be bound to leave the direction of foreign affairs in the hands of the Crown is that "force is supreme" in foreign affairs, and the military force of the nation is at the sole disposal of the Crown. Here is another riddle, but it is one which is hardly worth solving. Force is no more supreme in foreign than in domestic affairs. In one sense it is the backbone of all government. It is kept in reserve to enforce the will of the community when it is resisted, and is as really present in the arrest of a pickpocket as in the preparations for a campaign. As for the assertion that the military force of the nation is at the sole disposal of the Crown, it is playing with words. The military force of the nation belongs to the nation, which cannot be deprived of

it even for six weeks, except by fraud. The most important
point that can arise in foreign affairs is to determine when
moral effort shall give way to the use of force, and to say,
as the Reviewer does, that this is to be settled mainly by
the personal judgment and will of the Sovereign is to claim
for the crown a perilous prerogative—a prerogative so
perilous that the Crown could hardly be expected to
survive its frequent use. This is what I meant by saying
in one of my former letters that "the Crown we only
know as the ceremonial device of the Great Seal by which
the nation's resolves are attested, and the moment we
are forced to know it in any other capacity, danger
commences for one party, though hardly for both."
The "party" for whom danger would commence is, of
course, the Crown, for it is absurd to suppose that the
nation would long permit the Crown to play the autocrat
with its lives and fortunes, and as the nation is immeasurably the stronger of the two it would certainly issue
victoriously out of a struggle for existence. The Reviewer
gives one reason more in support of his doctrine. The
policy of England, he says, is one of non-intervention, but
while the principles of that policy are clear enough they
are difficult to apply. We have to steer our way "between
the Scylla of Absolutism and the Charybdis of Anarchy,"
and we can only hope to do so with safety "by leaving to
the Executive—we will go. further," says the Reviewer,
"and add the Sovereign herself—just liberty in the conduct
of foreign affairs." The main difficulty lies in knowing
when to intervene, and the nation is said to be disqualified

for deciding on this point because of its popular sympa
thies. If it had its way, Absolutism would stand no chance.
If an oppressed race rose in arms against its tormentors,
Englishmen everywhere would throw up their caps, and
demand that the influence of this country should be exerted
in favour of the insurgents. "French revolutionists, Spanish
juntas, Italian republicans, Hungarian rebels, Polish patriots,"
Englishmen have applauded them all by turns. In the same
mad way they have lately gone in for Servians, Bosnians,
Herzegovinians, Bulgarians, and Greeks in their struggle
with the Turk. For the last eighty years Englishmen have
been always sinning, and in their intemperate zeal for "civil
and religious liberty all the world over," there is no telling
what freak they may not commit. Hence they are utterly
unfit for taking any part in the guidance of foreign affairs.
The Crown is free from these weaknesses. It is severely
impartial, and knows how to hold the balance even between
rulers who presume too much upon their power, and subjects who are seized with too keen an enthusiasm for
freedom. The people are prejudiced. Possibly they would
have spurned alliance with the Emperor Napoleon so soon
after the horrors which Victor Hugo has lately painted, and
in that case there would have been no Crimean War. But
see how nicely the Queen managed him; how adroitly she
and the Prince twisted him round their fingers, and what
glorious results followed at Balaclava and Sebastopol. It
has been regarded by some persons as an open question
whether they twisted the Emperor round their fingers or
the Emperor twisted them round his, but loyalty admits of

but one reply.   However that may be, it is certain that the same " just liberty in the conduct of foreign affairs" which got us into one war would probably get us into another war of an equally glorious description, if the nation would only stand aside and trust the safety and honour of the State to the unadvised and irresponsible sagacity of the Crown.   This is what we are asked to do, but, notwithstanding the blandishments of the *Quarterly* Reviewer, I fancy the reply of the nation will be, " Not yet."

No. VII.

JUNE 8TH, 1878.

IT is time to end this discussion, the length of which may have unduly taxed the patience of my readers, but as this is my last letter I venture to hope that they will extend their goodness to my closing observations. My reply would have been much shorter if I had simply confined myself to rebutting the Reviewer's arguments. Nothing would have been easier than to ·"crumple him up," as the saying is. But apart from the distaste I have for mere logical controversy, grounded to a large extent upon a conviction of its uselessness except as pastime, I was anxious to listen to him, and to induce my readers to listen to him, so that we might together grasp the full import of what he was trying to say. For this purpose I have sought to give to his statements of fact and doctrine a completeness which they certainly did not possess as they left his pen; to lay hold of the principles he flourished for our acceptance, and to show them up as the malefactors and impostors they truly are. And this task I have undertaken as a mere matter of duty—a duty which has accidentally lighted upon my shoulders, but which is common to all Englishmen who have a head to think and a heart to feel, who know enough of the history of their country to cherish a patriotic pride in its chequered but glorious fortunes, and who scorn the notion of surrendering their blood-bought liberties into the hands of sophists and charlatans. So, as one of them, I render this poor but loving piece of service to the Commonwealth.

and, having done it, shall mix again with the citizen crowd among whom my sympathies and aspirations lie, and whose honest and uncorrupted thoughts I have striven to express. Did the occasion require this effort? Has the protest been raised too soon or made in tones too loud? Am I to be charged with taking affright at shadows and wasting my indignation upon men of straw? It is seldom wise to revile or disparage an opponent. In the present instance courtesy and loyalty would check any tendency to defame. My criticisms were first provoked by the " Life of the Prince Consort." The writer of that " Life " is not more than adequately described as " an accomplished man of letters," and we know it as a fact that an august personage supplies materials for his pen, and deigns to supervise his labours. For almost three-quarters of a century the *Quarterly Review* has been the literary organ of one of the two great political parties in the State. It exists for no other reason than to teach the influential classes of this country what they ought to think and how they ought to act in political matters. I do not know whether a politician conducts this important organ now, or who has the guardianship of the pipes that connect it with the intellect of the party, but it is highly significant that the tune it has just been playing is the same that was struck up a few months before by the instrumentalists at Windsor. The Reviewer catches up one by one the strange notes which were first heard there, and re-echoes them all, with many an assonant variation. But we have to deal with facts as well as words, with innovations wrought out in deeds as

well as expounded and recommended in dulcet writing.
The Administration of the Earl of Beaconsfield could hardly
have been other than it has been if the noble Israelite had
subscribed to the constitutional theories of Baron Stockmar
when he took the oath of office. As a writer in the *Journal
des Débats* observes, in criticising my former pamphlet, it is
only by occasional indiscretions, or by still rarer revelations,
that we know anything of what passes between the Crown
and the Cabinet; but if it were proper to apply the maxims
of the inductive sciences to the recent acts of Lord Beaconsfield's Administration, we should be led to the conclusion that some such theory of the Constitution as the
redoubtable Baron Stockmar elaborated, and the *Quarterly*
Reviewer has since defended, has been adopted by the
Premier as a code of working rules, and that we are now
living under the Constitution as it issued, revised, amended,
and extended, from the brain of the Prince Consort's adviser
and King Leopold's pensioner. Constitutional questions as
affecting the relations between the Crown and Parliament
are happily not of very frequent occurrence, but there have
been three such questions within the last four years, and
two within the last three months. Knowing nothing directly
of what takes place behind the curtained penetralia of the
Executive, and shut up to such inferences as can be drawn
from the acts of Government, one would say that the Queen
has entered upon the part which she allowed to be ascribed
to her as of right in the " Life of the Prince Consort," that
she is already quietly recognised by her Ministers as the
permanent Premier of the Cabinet, and that the foreign

E

affairs of the country at the present momentous crisis are
settled between her and the Earl of Beaconsfield. There
is no hardihood, there is no presumption in hazarding
such conjectures. The facts we observe appear to warrant
them, and facts are sacred. The theory they assume has
been presented to us under the literary sign-manual of
the Queen herself. The constitutional delicacy which at
one time might have seemed to be strained and sullied
by mentioning them has been denounced under the
shadow of the same august authority as savouring of latent
Republicanism, and indicative of principles which can only
attain fruition by the downfall of the Monarchy. It therefore seems to be her Royal will that we should recognise
her hand in the phenomena of the political heavens, and
speak of her with as much openness and as little ceremony
as we use in speaking of her Ministers. A long course of
pious habit made me slow to use the privilege; but when
events conspire with the Royal will to compel us either to
speak or to suffer wrong, then I yield to compulsion, I seize
the privilege as a right, and act accordingly. So I ask
again, putting all these facts together, is not the present
Constitutional crisis one that not only merits and warrants
but imperatively demands the use I have made of it? Are
we to go on sleeping while we know that an enemy is privily
sowing tares in our fathers' wheatcrofts? Are we to remain
dumb while the Constitution is travestied before our eyes,
and writers who would at one time have been called venal
try to mystify us with their special pleading and to argue
us out of our birthright? Nothing less than this is intended

if we accept the authority of the Reviewer, and some of the means he suggests are remarkable. Baron Stockmar had already urged that, "as matters now stand, the necessary equilibrium of the Constitution can only be established and maintained by throwing a well-merited and deeply-seated popularity on the side of the Sovereign into the scale against the Democratic element which has become so powerful in the House of Commons." The old man, with a delicacy which the countrymen of Goethe may appreciate, even ventured to maintain that the House of Lords had found a safeguard against the wild power of Democracy in "the moral purity" of the Queen. The Reviewer descends to more trivial particulars. He enumerates the "number of farmers" who rode with the Royal party through Dunstable in 1841, nearly "smothering them with dust." He refers to what took place at the distribution of the Crimean medals to the first batch of returned veterans, when " from the highest Prince of the blood to the lowest private, all received the same distinction for the bravest conduct in the severest actions, and the rough hand of the brave and honest private soldier came for the first time in contact with that of their Sovereign and their Queen." This is an extract from one of the Queen's letters to the King of the Belgians, and the Reviewer cries out in ecstacy, "Let those who think that all feudal feeling is extinct in England read this." Even smaller acts of Royal kindness are not deemed too insignificant to be dwelt upon. He tells us that "many a widow of a lost miner, or a drowned sailor, has been cheered by the expression of Her Majesty's sympathy with her suffering ; many a hero of humble station has exulted at the thought that his conduct has merited the notice and approval of his Sovereign." The Reviewer is well fitted to follow in the footsteps of Baron Stockmar with his "moral purity." I marvel greatly at his taste, but I marvel more at the invidious light in which he seeks to place the most ordinary expressions of the Queen's kindheartedness. We all know the goodness of her nature. We know how keenly she feels when any of her subjects suffer under exceptionally severe calamities, and when the newspapers tell us of the kind inquiries she has made, or of the marks of sympathy she has shown, we say to ourselves that it is like the Queen, and that it is very good of her. But the Reviewer contrives to take the bloom off these gracious acts. He reduces them to the level of a mercantile transaction, and finds a place for them in the Constitution. They help to construct a barrier against Democracy. They are so much fuel to be put into the boiler of loyalty for getting up the steam. They are like the arts by which children are humoured in order to be ruled. They belong to the machinery of Imperialism, the essence of which consists in adopting, not from kindness, but from calculation, the ways of an indulgent father or a rich uncle, so that the people may be merry in their chains and induced to kiss the rod. In the words of the Reviewer, those acts of Royal kindness, and the demonstrations of loyalty which everywhere attend the Queen, indicate "a perpetual gravitation of the Crown and the people towards each other, tending to close up the breach that was made in the Royal authority by the Revolution." All roads lead to London, and so even by these idyllic footpaths, strewn with the blossoms of Royal compassion, we are led back to the problem which German medico-philosophers, accomplished men of letters, eloquent *Quarterly* Reviewers, and scheming statesmen with their hands on the helm of power are endeavouring to work out, the problem being how most effectually and with the least noise to roll back the history of England two hundred years. The task they have undertaken is, "to close up the breach that was made in the Royal authority by the Revolution;" that is, to make the authority of our Kings and Queens what it was before it was broken in upon and curtailed, for their benefit and for ours, by the Bill of Rights and the Act of Settlement. The proposal itself has a sinister look for the present dynasty. The Queen is asked to recur to the political principles of a period when the title-deeds by which she reigns had not been made out, and to violate the terms upon which the estate is held. Her ancestors were offered the Crown of England upon certain express conditions; they accepted it subject to those conditions, and we are now told that we must annul the conditions, and render the ownership absolute. Of course, if the contract were to be broken, both parties would resume their rights, and a Convention of 1880 might have to take up the lapsed work of the Convention of 1689. But it is all moonshine. The doctrines of the Reviewer are treasonable, but they are also impracticable, and that is a good deal better. The course of the Constitution since 1688 has not been one of deterioration, but of regular and natural development, and it can no more be changed into what it was then than a river can be made to flow back towards its source. The last of the Stuarts used to touch for the King's Evil. The prerogative of healing scrofula appertained to the Crown of England for six hundred years, and was only lost by the Revolution, when the transfer of the Crown from the legitimate to another line was supposed to have destroyed the charm. This lost prerogative will be restored whenever the rest are restored. Happily the people of England have a distaste for violent changes. They love the past, and instead of breaking with it they want to carry it along with them into the days that are to come. The force of events, springing out of and controlled by the national character, has transformed our ancient Monarchy into a form of government only in one respect distinguishable from a Republic. It is a Crowned Republic. It has its elected presidents, its First Ministers, who receive from time to time the mandates of the nation, who do the hard and responsible work of Government, and in time give place to others; but above them there is a continuing Sovereignty, so styled as a mark of honour; a King or Queen, who under our settled law reigns by hereditary right. Who would wish to be blind to, or seek to quench, the lustre which surrounds that title, the noblest and most illustrious borne by any potentate on earth? We love to adorn the wearer of it with all possible perfections, to see graciousness in his smile and benignity in his actions. If he has any faults we try not to see them, and we resent with a touch of wounded affection any conduct on his part that clashes with the fiction of his blame-lessness. We honour him as representing the unity, the greatness, and the majesty of the nation ; as a living symbol of authority and law; as the last link in a grand historic chain of renowned names and stately reputations, which connects the England of to-day with its rude beginnings, and helps us to feel our oneness with the famous men of old. Such is the case now, and such it may be for a period so long that no one can pretend to foresee its close, if the spirit of the compact between Crown and People is faithfully observed, and reasonableness gives free scope to the modify-ing and mellowing influences of time. Is this position one that needs aggrandising to make it worthy of an occupier ? Is it one which a Queen who respects herself cannot deign to fill with utter fidelity to its attendant limits and condi-tions ? I believe not, I trust not, for in spite of what theorists may say I love to move on quietly, without being disturbed by auguries of revolution. It is out of this loyalty that I have spoken. My aim is to deprecate revolutionary changes, not to provoke them. But my love of freedom is greater than my fear of change, and I am of those who agree to follow her at all risks. In the meantime only those are loyal who venture to tell the truth. Flattery is always false and base, but the State itself has need to take warning when it is uttered or acted too near the Throne, and next to having a noble-minded and gracious Queen, the greatest blessing for which we ought to pray is that Heaven may always send her honest men to guide her counsels.